james blunt

back to bedlam

Arranging and engraving: Artemis Music Limited
(www.artemismusic.com)

Published 2004

High

Words and Music by James Blunt and Ricky Ross

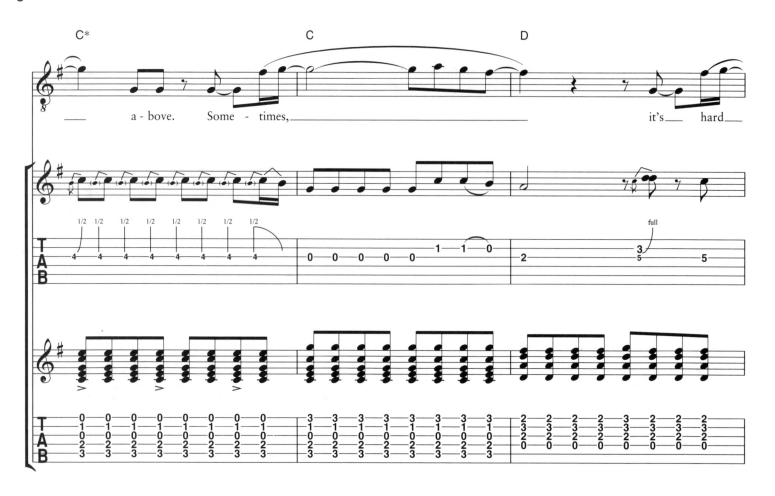

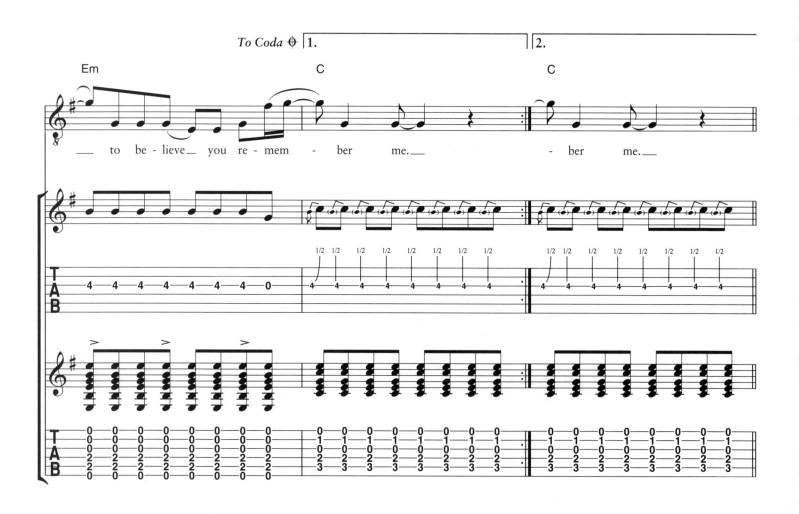

Bridge

Will you be___ my shoul-der, when I'm grey___ and old - er?

Pro-mise me___ to-mor-row starts_____ with you. Get-ting high___

Coda

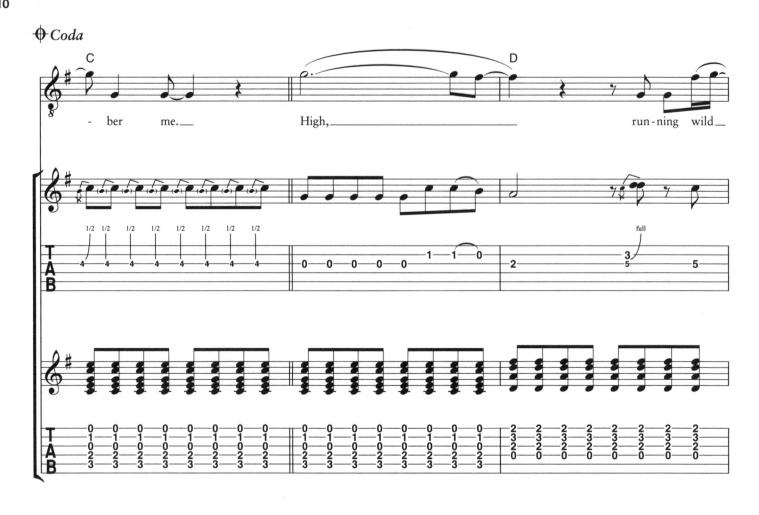

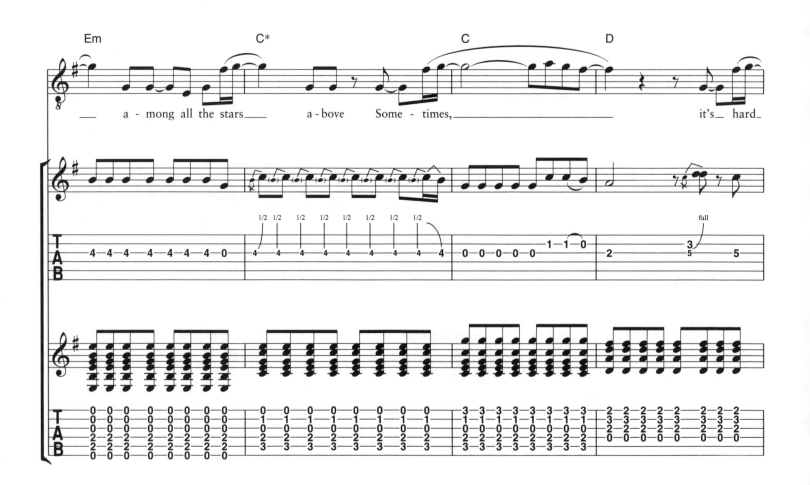

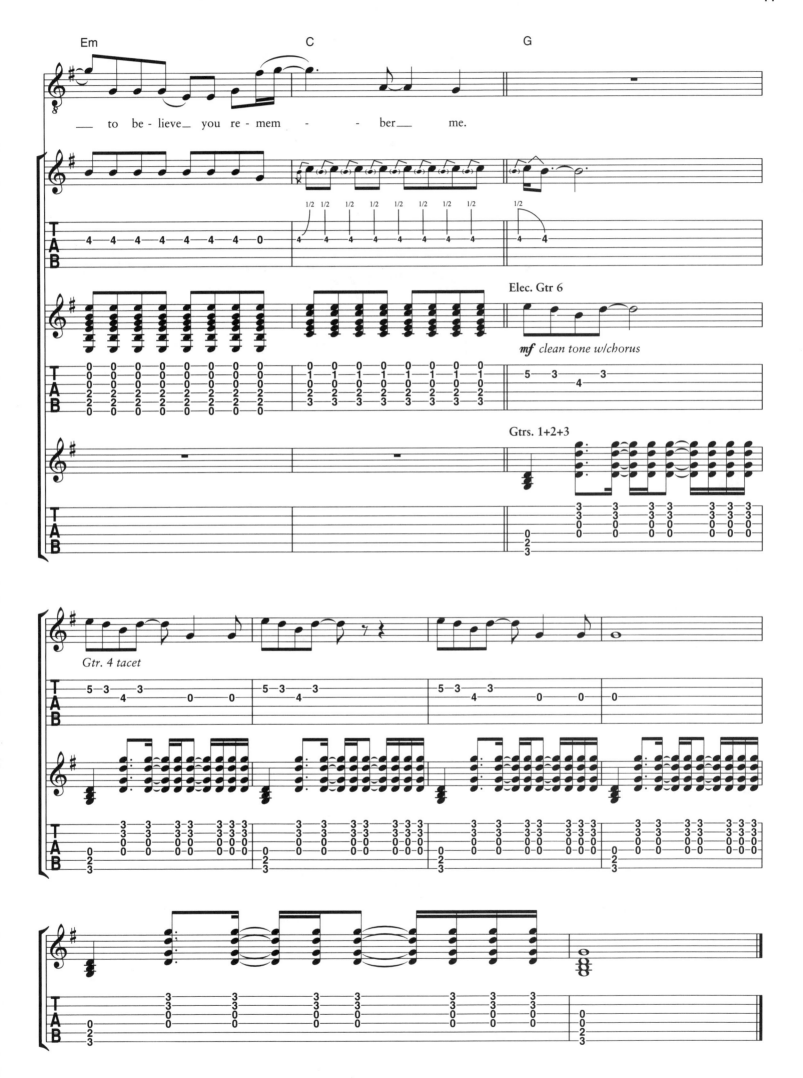

You're Beautiful

Words and Music by James Blunt, Sacha Skarbek and Amanda Ghost

Chorus

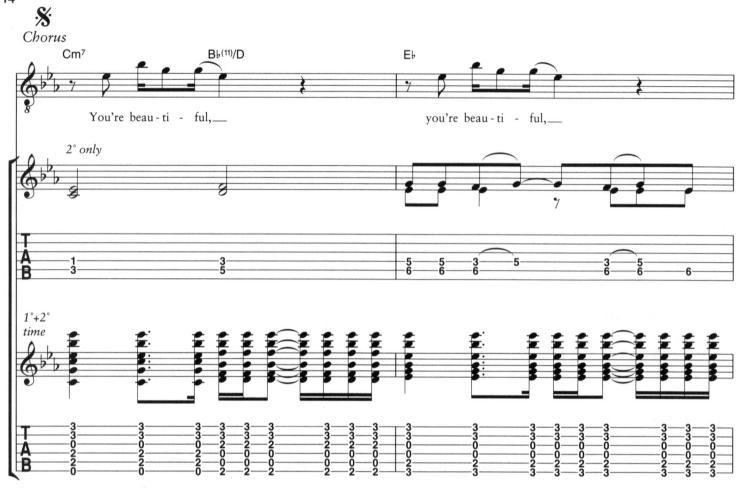

You're beau - ti - ful,___ you're beau - ti - ful,___

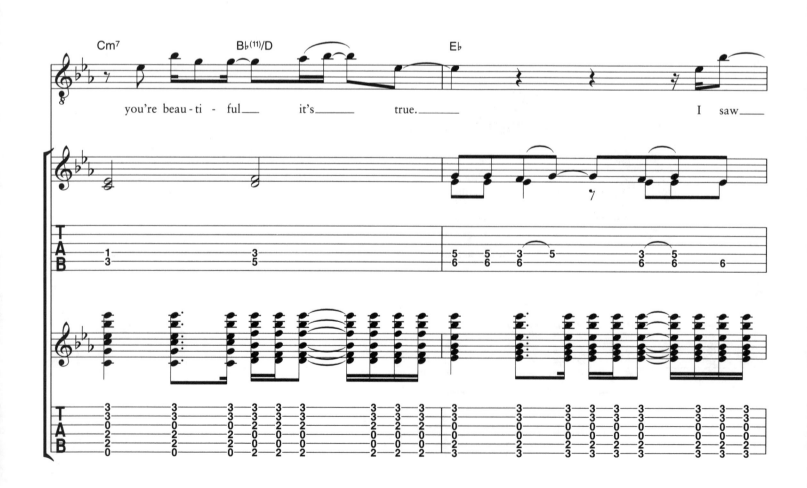

you're beau - ti - ful___ it's_____ true._____ I saw____

Chorus

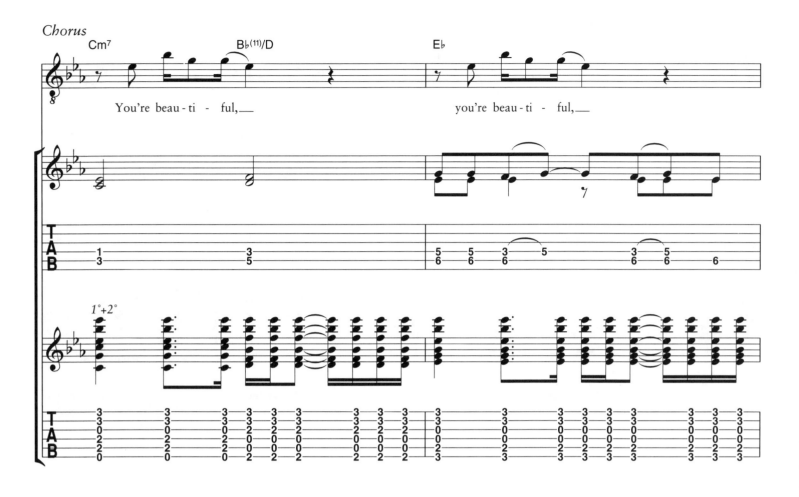

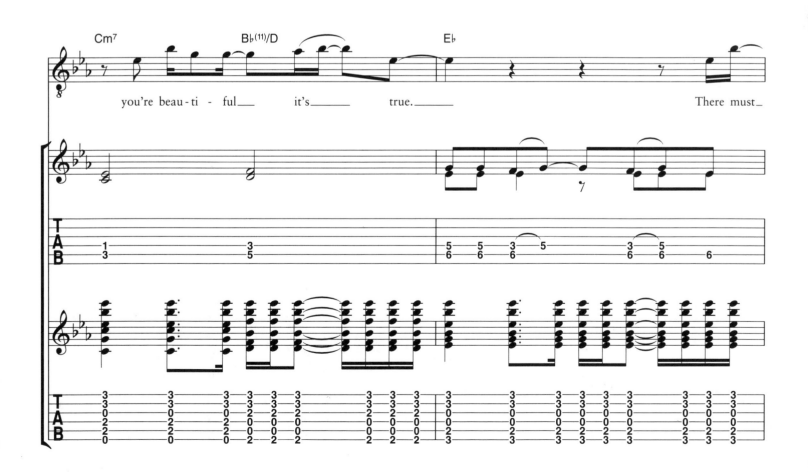

18

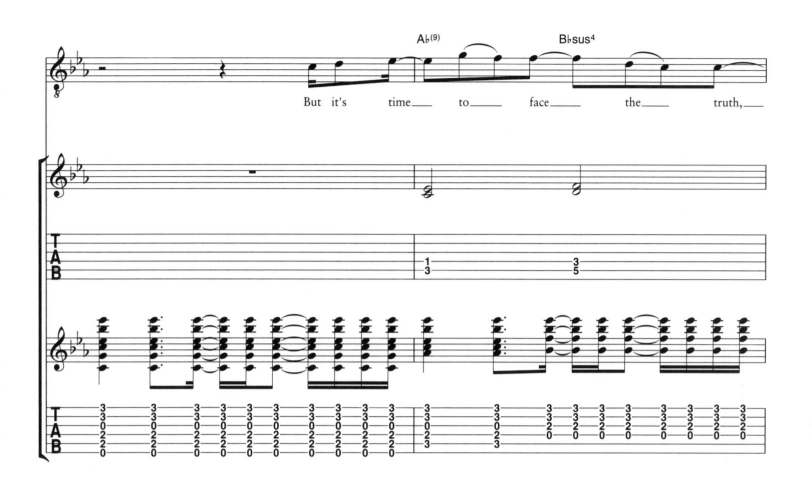

But it's time____ to____ face____ the____ truth,____

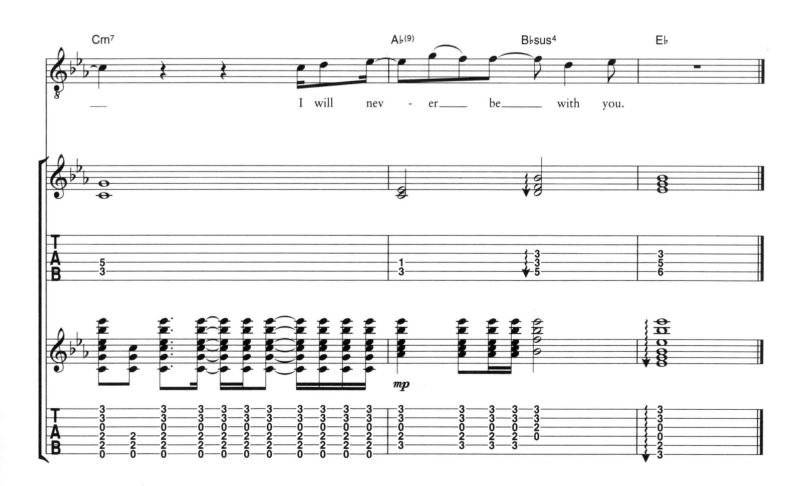

I will nev - er____ be____ with you.

Wisemen

Words and Music by James Blunt, Jimmy Hogarth and Sacha Skarbek

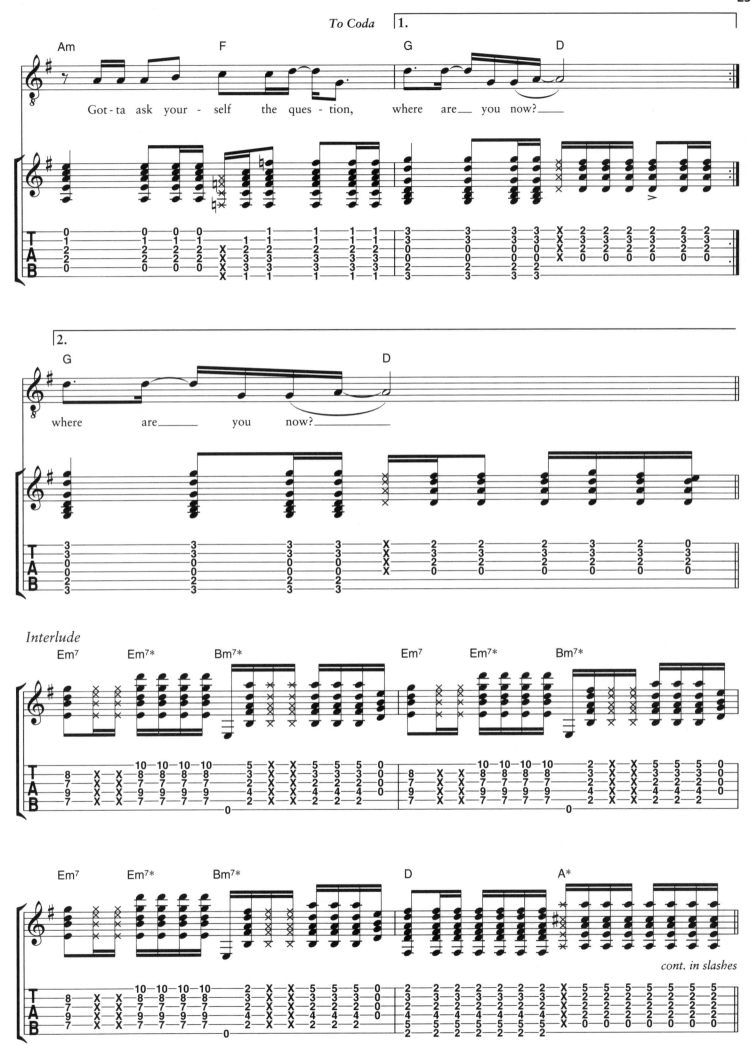

To Coda | 1.

Am   F   G   D

Got-ta ask your-self the ques-tion, where are___ you now?___

2.

G   D

where are___ you now?___

Interlude

Em⁷ Em⁷* Bm⁷* Em⁷ Em⁷* Bm⁷*

Em⁷ Em⁷* Bm⁷* D   A*

cont. in slashes

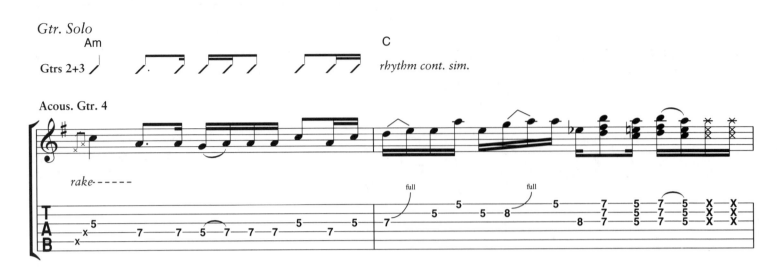

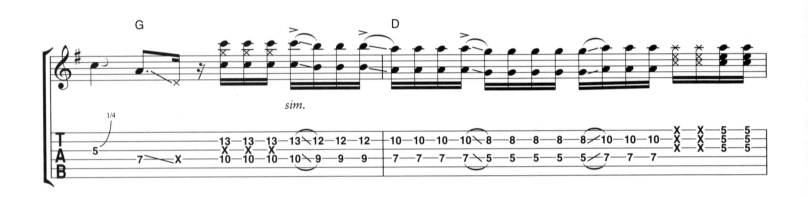

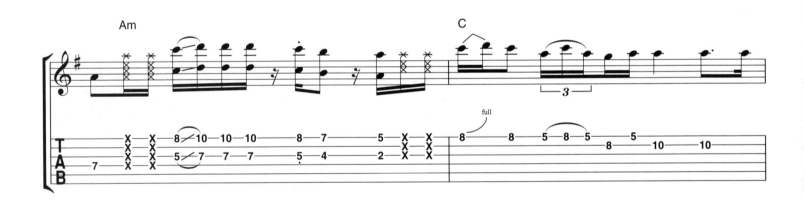

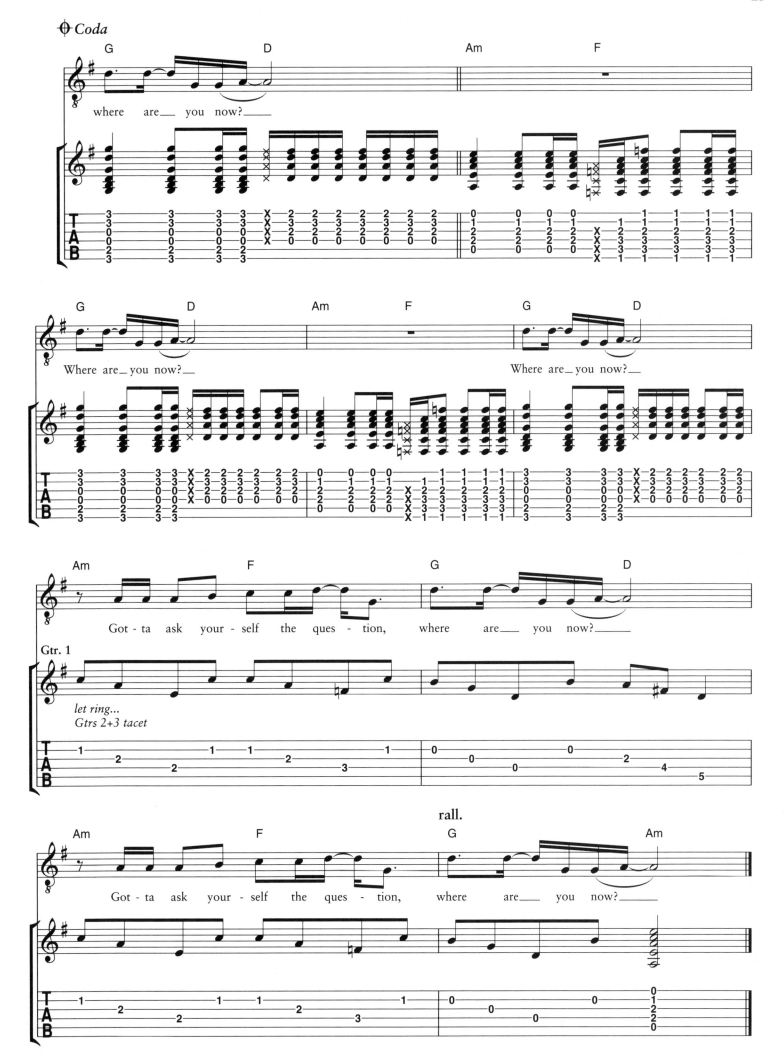

Goodbye My Lover

Words and Music by James Blunt and Sacha Skarbek

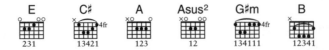

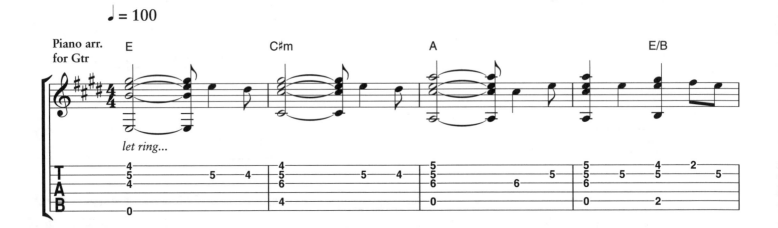

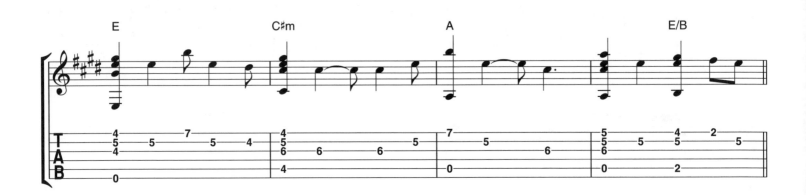

1. Did I dis-ap-point_ you,_ or let you down?_ Should I be feel-ing guilt-y,

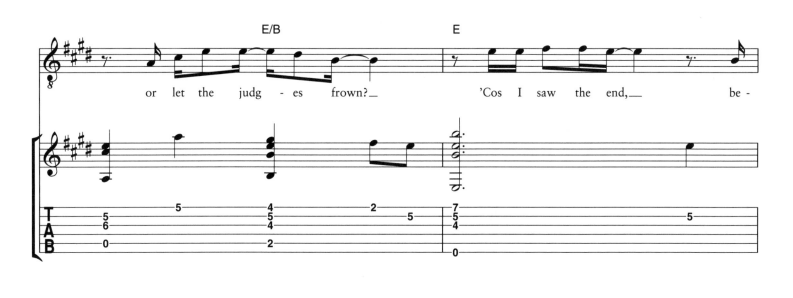

or let the judg-es frown?__ 'Cos I saw the end,__ be-

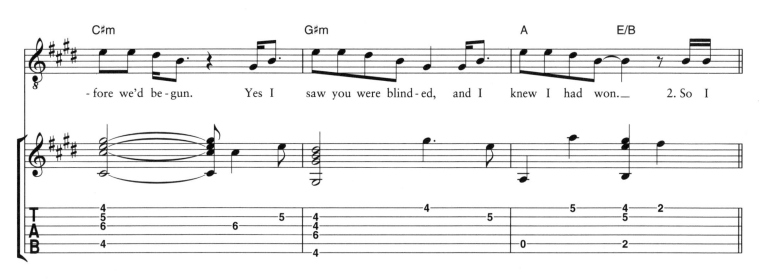

-fore we'd be-gun. Yes I saw you were blind-ed, and I knew I had won.__ 2. So I

Verse

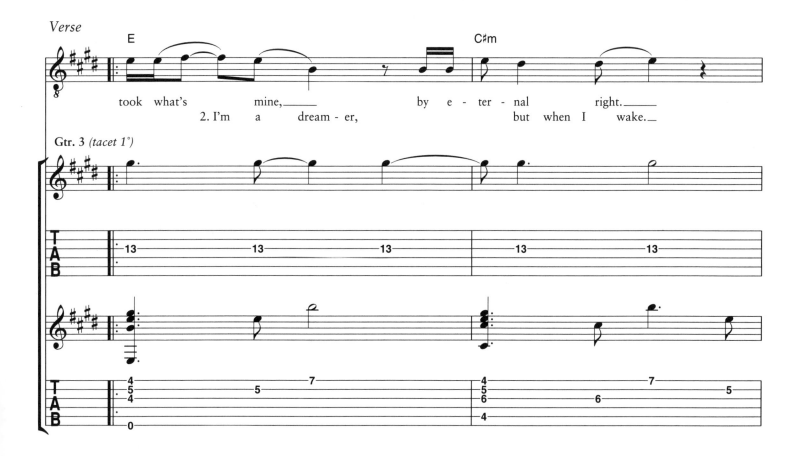

took what's mine,_____ by e-ter-nal right._____

2. I'm a dream-er, but when I wake.__

Gtr. 3 *(tacet 1°)*

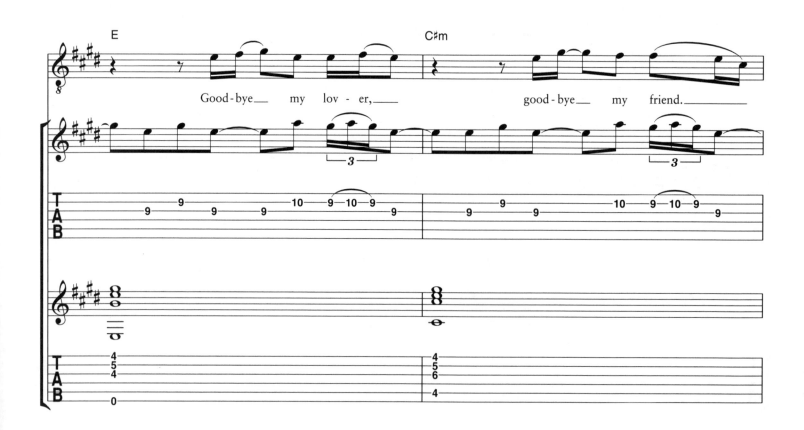

You have been_ the one,_ you have been_ the one for__ me.__

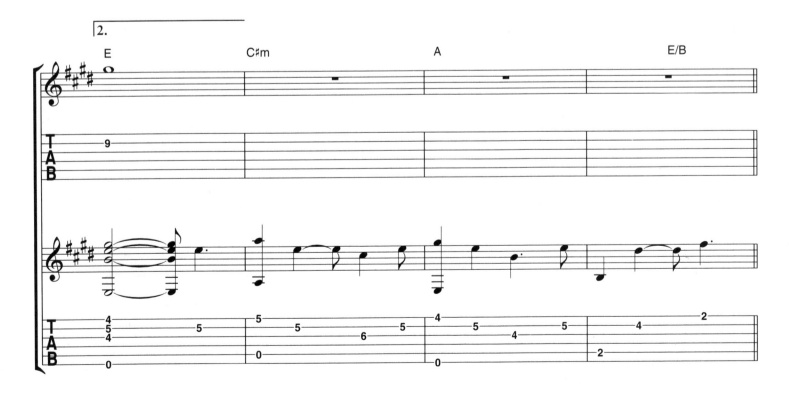

Bridge

And I still___ hold your_ hand_ in mine,___ in mine___ when I'm a-sleep.

D.%. al Coda

And I will___ bear my___ soul_ in time,___ When I'm kneel-ing at___ your___ feet.

Coda

___ I'm so___ hol-low ba - by,___ I'm so___ hol - low.___

Gtr. 1 *(tacet 1°)*

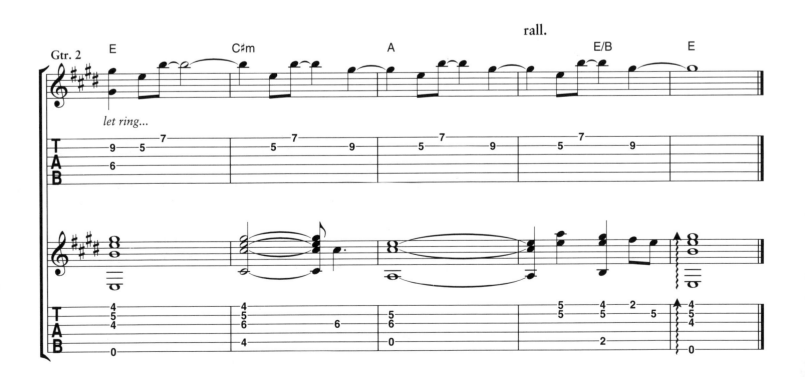

Tears And Rain

Words and Music by Guy Chambers and James Blunt

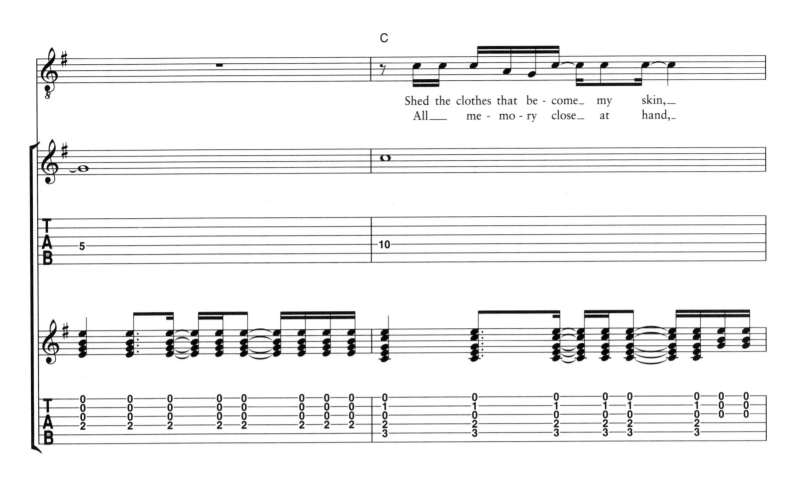

Shed the clothes that be - come_ my skin,_
All_ me - mo - ry close_ at hand,_

see a light that burns_with - in_ my need - ing.
help me_ un - der - stand_ the years._

...Fig 1 ends

How I wish I'd_ chos - en, the dark - ness from_ cold._
How I wish I could_ choose be - tween_ hea - ven and_ hell.

Elec. Gtr. 2

mf let ring...
w/clean tone

How I wish I'd screamed out loud,_ in - stead I found_ no mean -
How I wish I would save_ my soul,_ I'm so_ cold_ from fear._

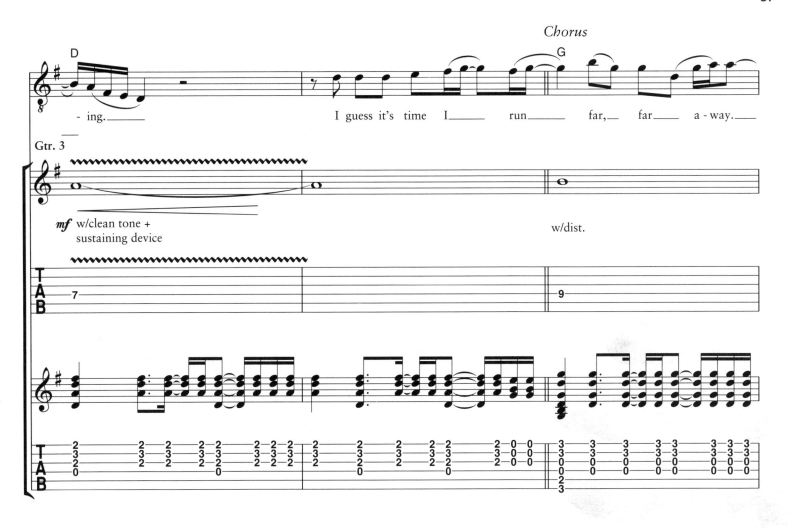

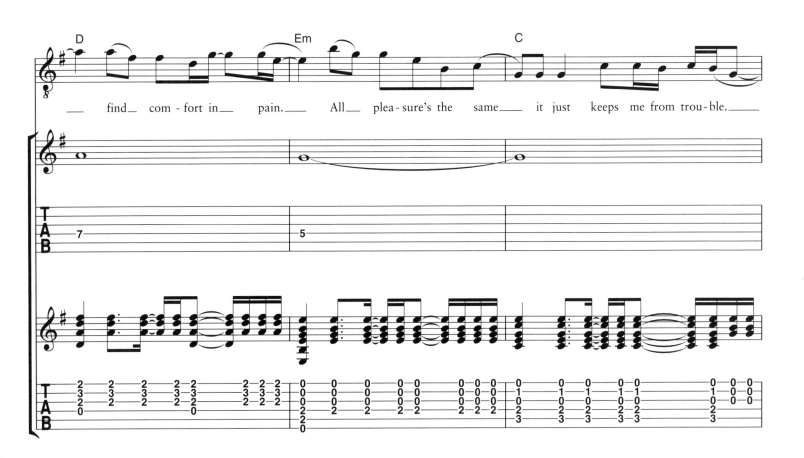

Hides_ my true_ shame,_ like Do - ri - an_ Gray,_ I've heard what they say._

1.

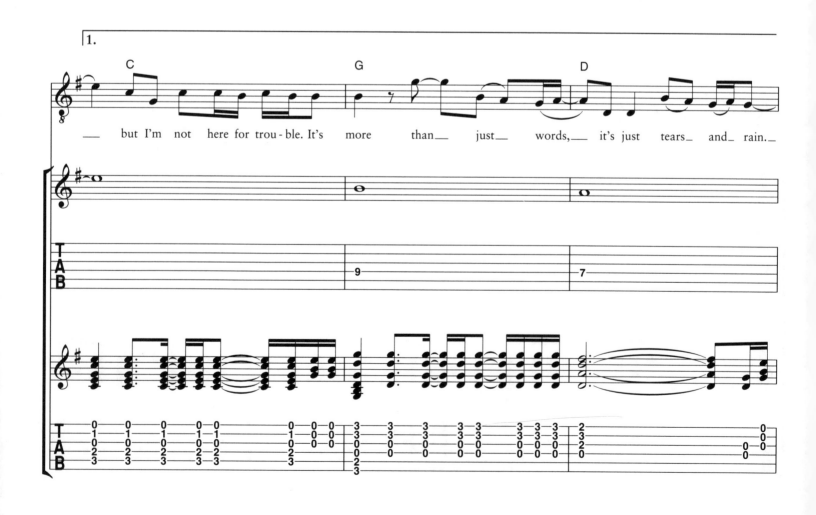

_ but I'm not here for trou - ble. It's more than_ just_ words,_ it's just tears_ and_ rain._

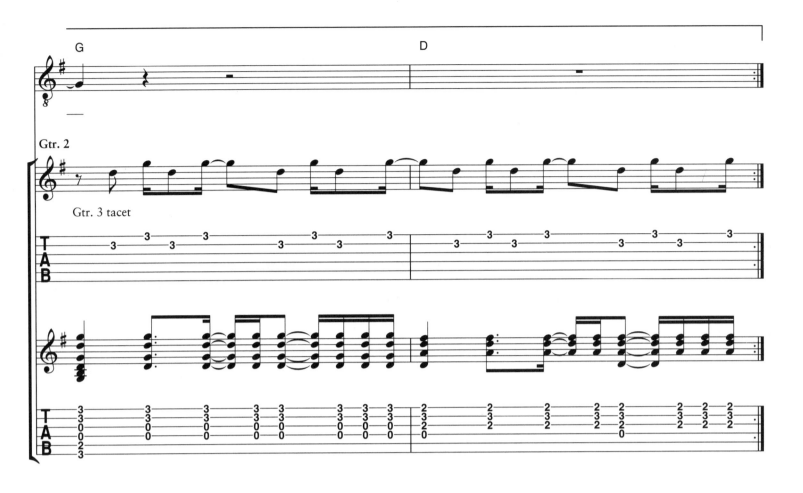

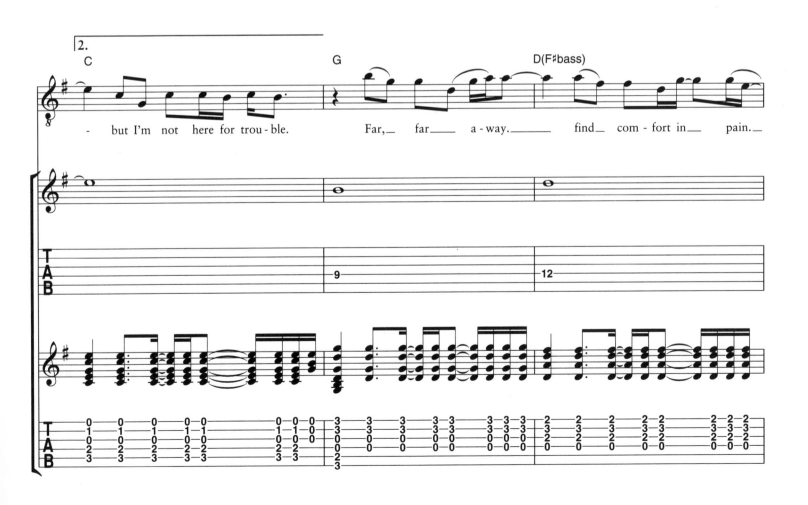

Out Of My Mind

Words and Music by James Blunt

All gtrs. capo 3rd fret

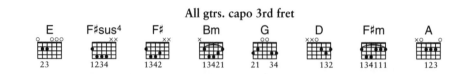

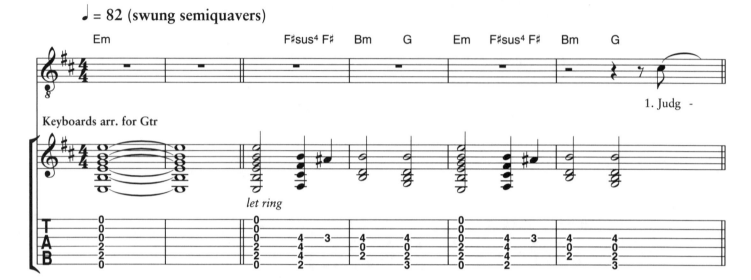

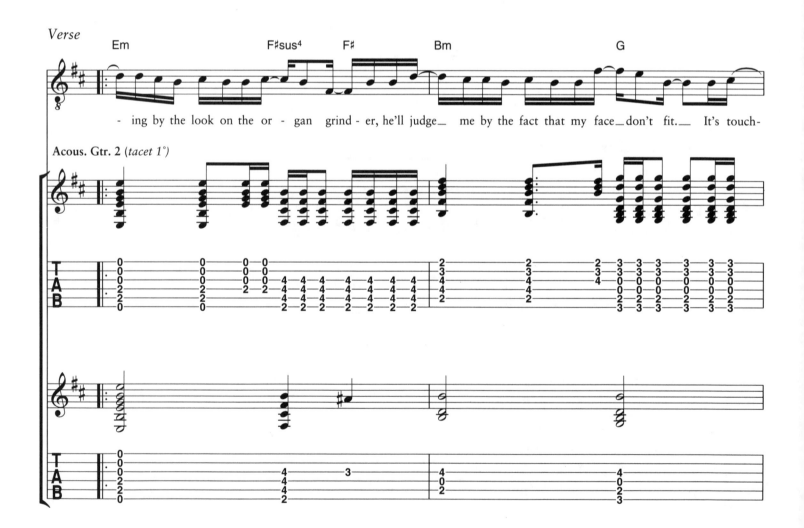

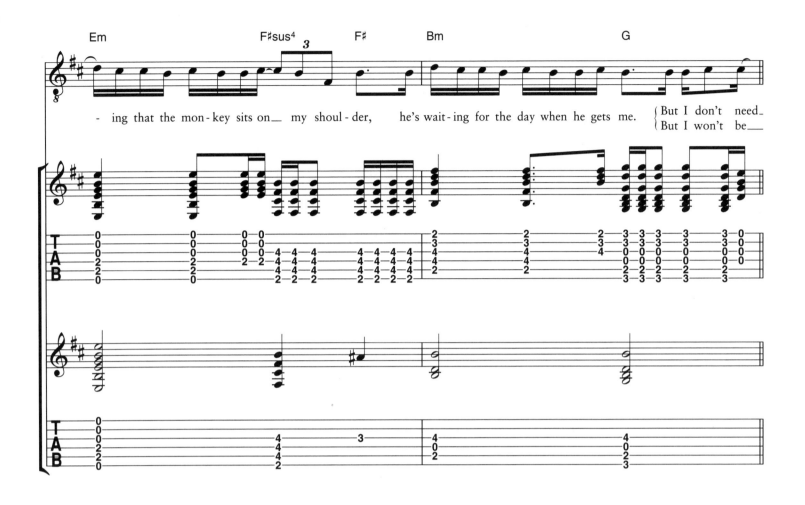

- ing that the mon-key sits on_ my shoul-der, he's wait-ing for the day when he gets me. {But I don't need_
{But I won't be_

Pre-Chorus

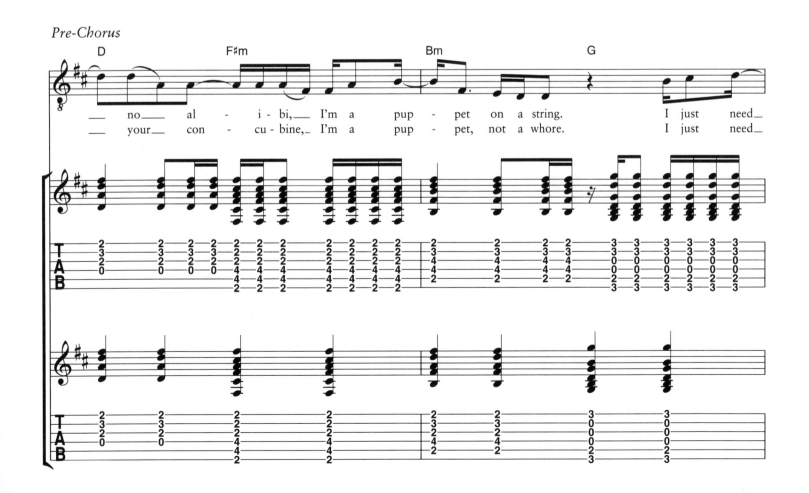

_ no _ al - i - bi,_ I'm a pup - pet on a string. I just need_
_ your _ con - cu - bine,_ I'm a pup - pet, not a whore. I just need_

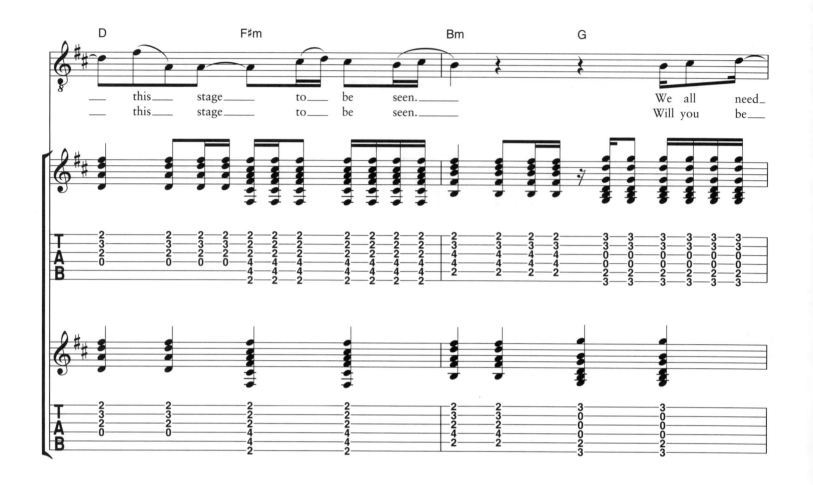

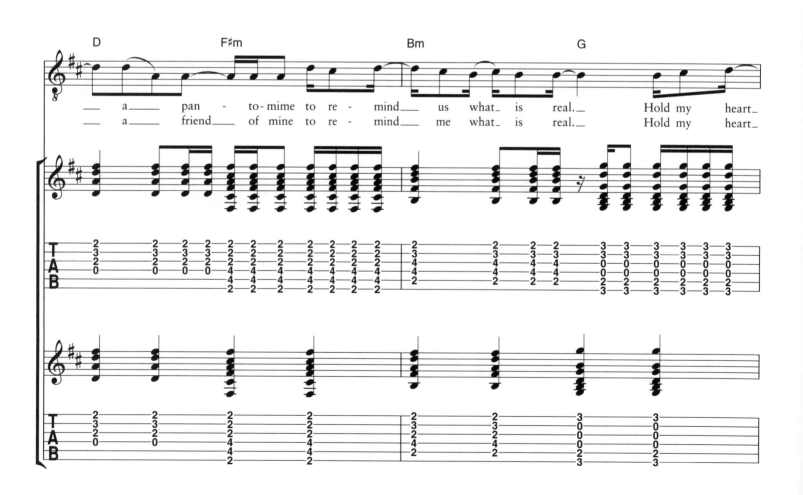

So Long, Jimmy

Words and Music by James Blunt and Jimmy Hogarth

chords implied by harmony

Gtr 3 tacet

Interlude

Organ arr. for Gtr.

Bass arr. for Gtr.

Gtr. 1

Gtr. Solo

Acous. Gtr. 4

Billy

Words and Music by James Blunt, Sacha Skarbek and Amanda Ghost

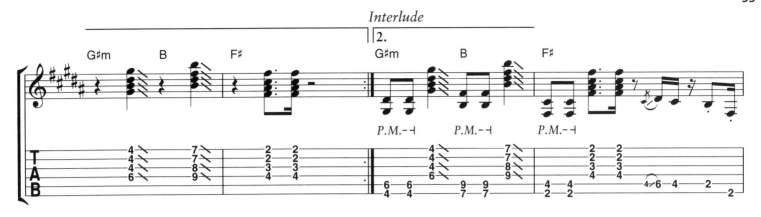

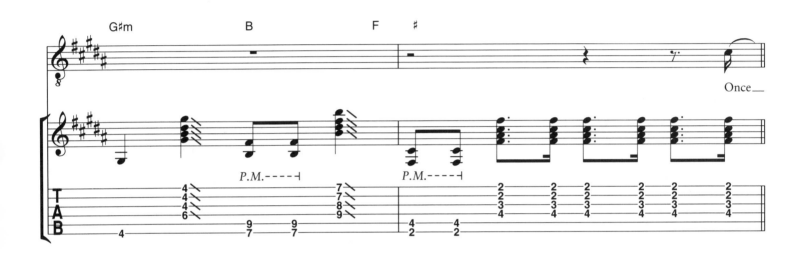

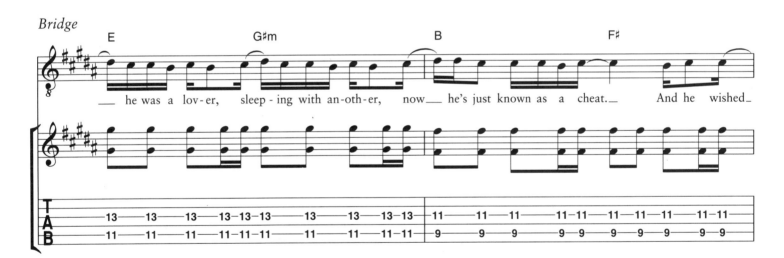

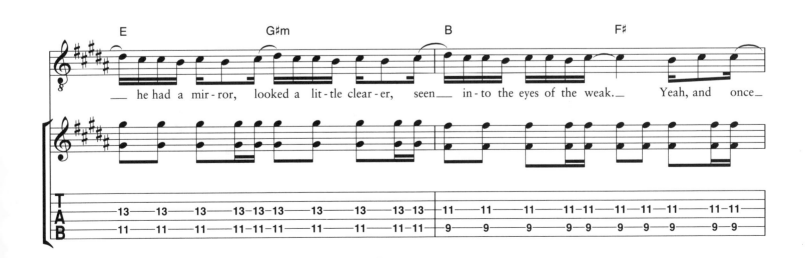

Cry

Words and Music by James Blunt and Sacha Skarbek

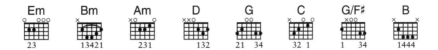

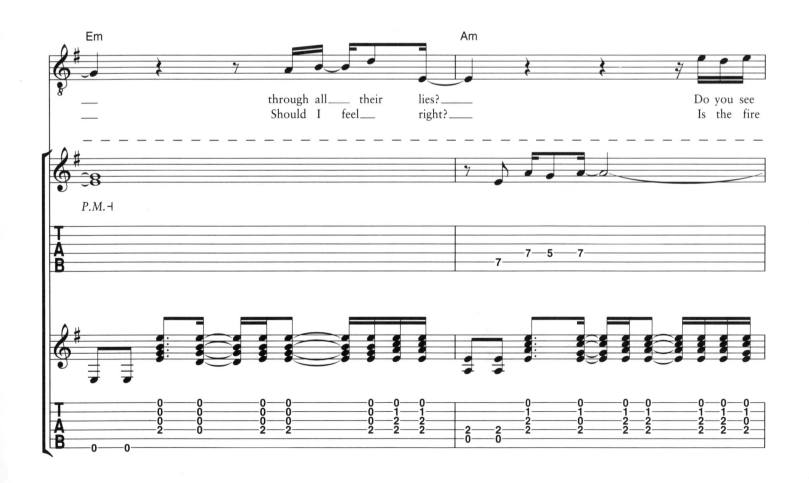

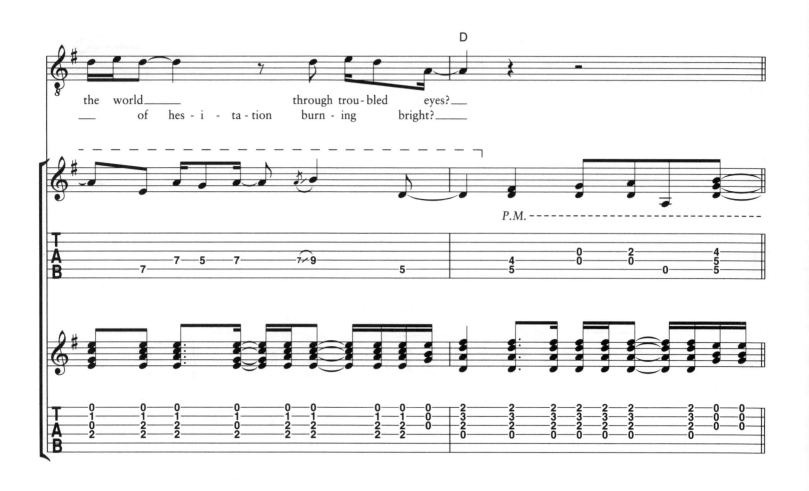

the world_____ through trou-bled eyes?____
____ of hes-i-ta-tion burn-ing bright?____

Chorus

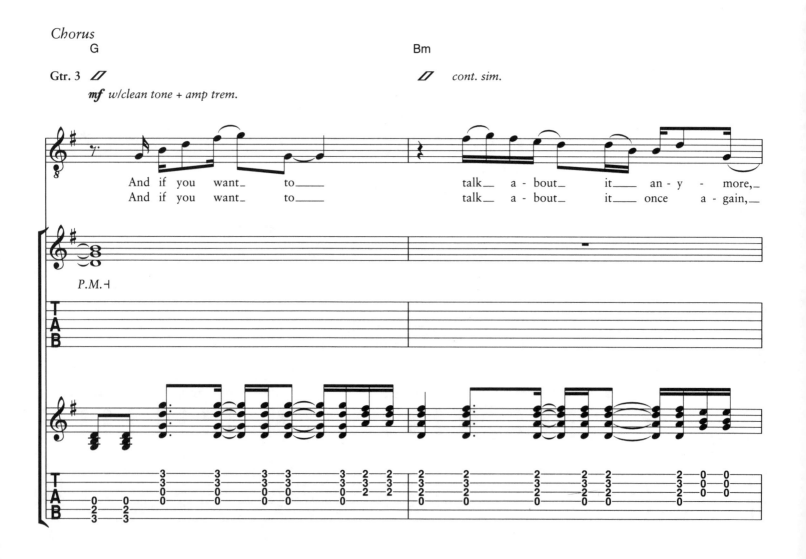

And if you want_ to_____ talk_ a-bout_ it____ an-y-more,_
And if you want_ to_____ talk_ a-bout_ it____ once a-gain,_

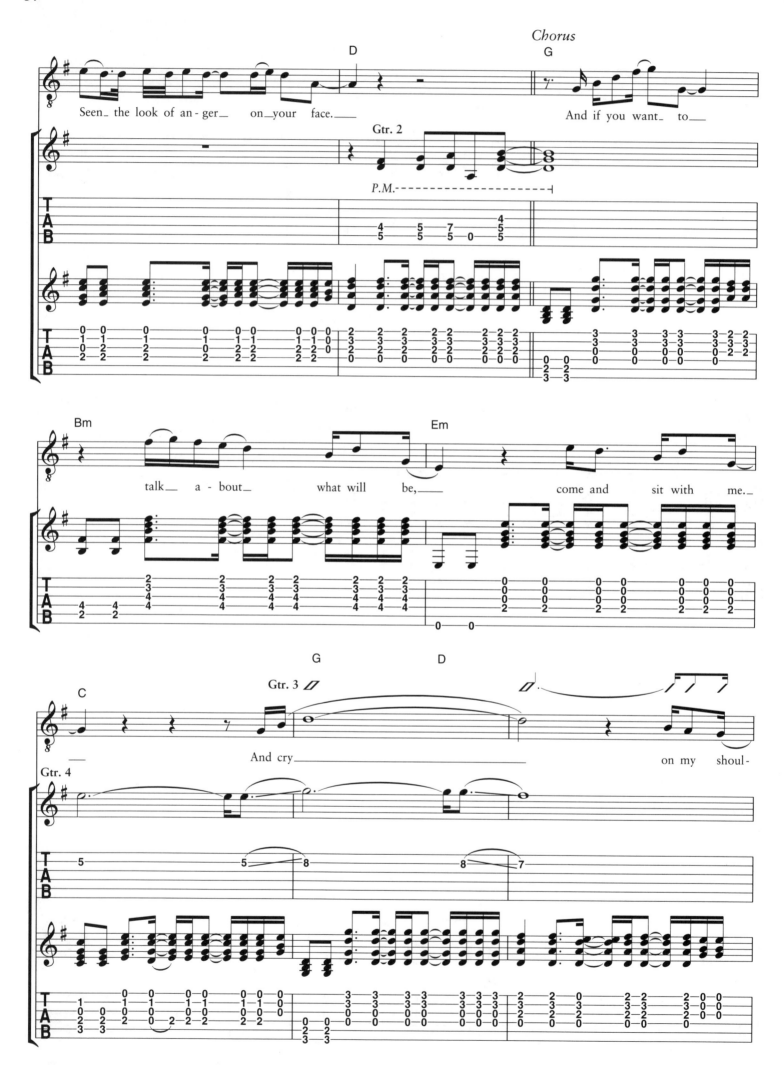

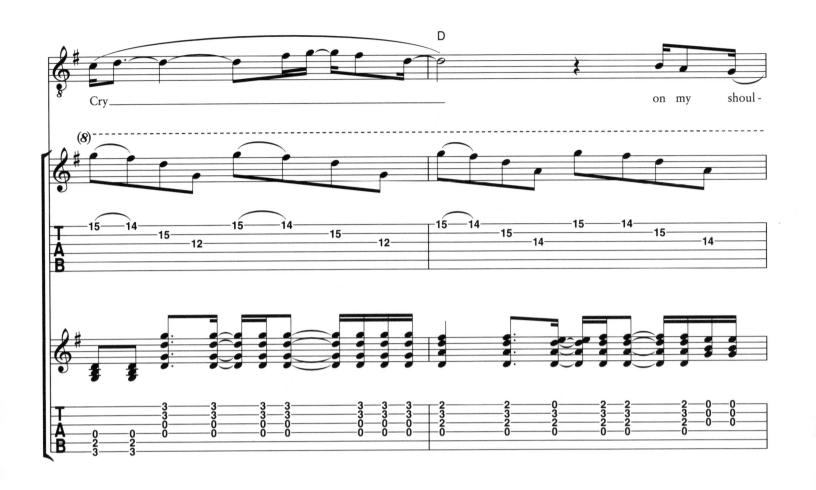

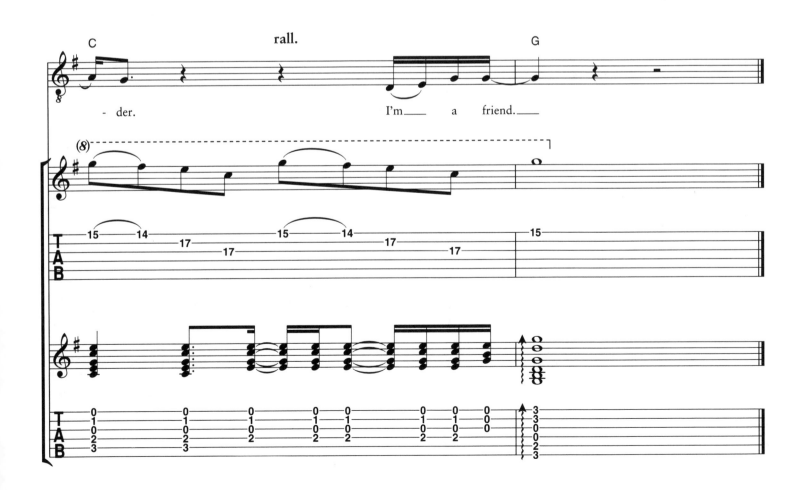

No Bravery

Words and Music by James Blunt and Sacha Skarbek

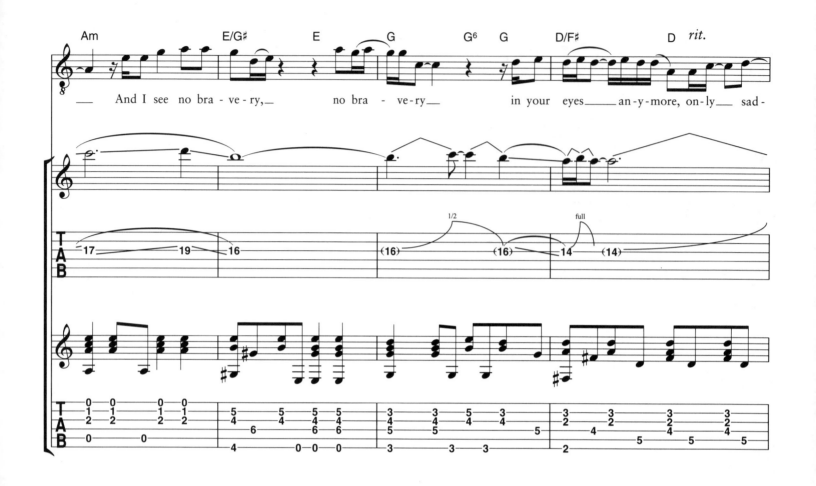

And I see no bra - ve - ry,___ no bra - ve - ry___ in your eyes___ an - y - more, on - ly___ sad-

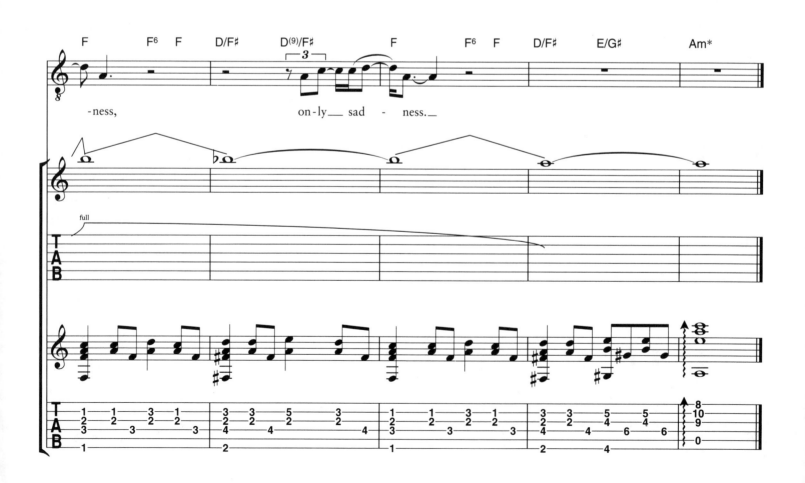

-ness, on - ly___ sad___ - ness.___

GUITAR TAB GLOSSARY**

TABLATURE EXPLANATION

READING TABLATURE: Tablature illustrates the six strings of the guitar. Notes and chords are indicated by the placement of fret numbers on a given string(s).

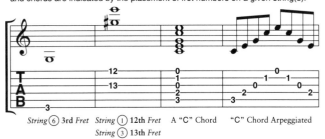

String ⑥ 3rd Fret *String ① 12th Fret* A "C" Chord "C" Chord Arpeggiated
String ③ 13th Fret

BENDING NOTES

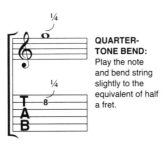

HALF STEP: Play the note and bend string one half step.*

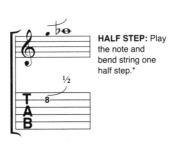

WHOLE STEP: Play the note and bend string one whole step.

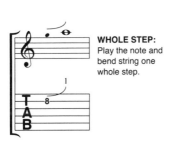

WHOLE STEP AND A HALF: Play the note and bend string a whole step and a half.

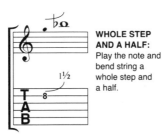

QUARTER-TONE BEND: Play the note and bend string slightly to the equivalent of half a fret.

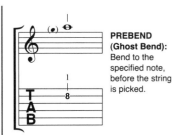

PREBEND (Ghost Bend): Bend to the specified note, before the string is picked.

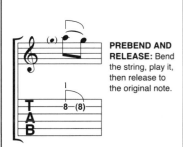

PREBEND AND RELEASE: Bend the string, play it, then release to the original note.

REVERSE BEND: Play the already-bent string, then immediately drop it down to the fretted note.

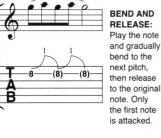

BEND AND RELEASE: Play the note and gradually bend to the next pitch, then release to the original note. Only the first note is attacked.

*A half step is the smallest interval in Western music; it is equal to one fret. A whole step equals two frets.

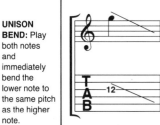

UNISON BEND: Play both notes and immediately bend the lower note to the same pitch as the higher note.

DOUBLE NOTE BEND: Play both notes and immediately bend both strings simultaneously.

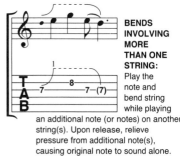

BENDS INVOLVING MORE THAN ONE STRING: Play the note and bend string while playing an additional note (or notes) on another string(s). Upon release, relieve pressure from additional note(s), causing original note to sound alone.

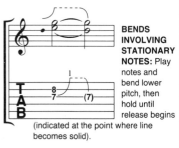

BENDS INVOLVING STATIONARY NOTES: Play notes and bend lower pitch, then hold until release begins (indicated at the point where line becomes solid).

TREMOLO BAR

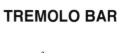
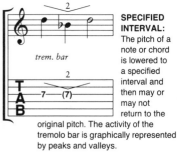

SPECIFIED INTERVAL: The pitch of a note or chord is lowered to a specified interval and then may or may not return to the original pitch. The activity of the tremolo bar is graphically represented by peaks and valleys.

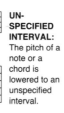

UN-SPECIFIED INTERVAL: The pitch of a note or a chord is lowered to an unspecified interval.

HARMONICS

NATURAL HARMONIC: A finger of the fret hand lightly touches the note or notes indicated in the tab and is played by the pick hand.

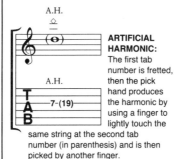

ARTIFICIAL HARMONIC: The first tab number is fretted, then the pick hand produces the harmonic by using a finger to lightly touch the same string at the second tab number (in parenthesis) and is then picked by another finger.

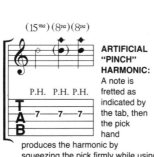

ARTIFICIAL "PINCH" HARMONIC: A note is fretted as indicated by the tab, then the pick hand produces the harmonic by squeezing the pick firmly while using the tip of the index finger in the pick attack. If parenthesis are found around the fretted note, it does not sound. No parenthesis means both the fretted note and A.H. are heard simultaneously.

**By Kenn Chipkin and Aaron Stang

RHYTHM SLASHES

STRUM INDICA-TIONS: Strum with indicated rhythm.

The chord voicings are found on the first page of the transcription underneath the song title.

SINGLE NOTES IN SLASH NOTATION: A regular notehead indicates a single note. The circled number below the note indicates which string of the chord to strike. If the note is not in the chord, the fret number will be indicated above the note(s).

ARTICULATIONS

HAMMER ON: Play lower note, then "hammer on" to higher note with another finger. Only the first note is attacked.

LEFT HAND HAMMER: Hammer on the first note played on each string with the left hand.

PULL OFF: Play higher note, then "pull off" to lower note with another finger. Only the first note is attacked.

FRET-BOARD TAPPING: "Tap" onto the note indicated by + with a finger of the pick hand, then pull off to the following note held by the fret hand.

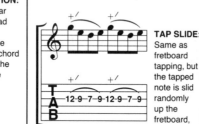

TAP SLIDE: Same as fretboard tapping, but the tapped note is slid randomly up the fretboard, then pulled off to the following note.

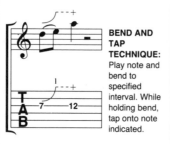

BEND AND TAP TECHNIQUE: Play note and bend to specified interval. While holding bend, tap onto note indicated.

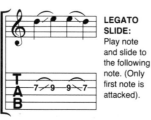

LEGATO SLIDE: Play note and slide to the following note. (Only first note is attacked).

LONG GLISSAN-DO: Play note and slide in specified direction for the full value of the note.

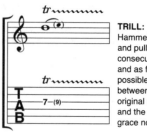

SHORT GLISSAN-DO: Play note for its full value and slide in specified direction at the last possible moment.

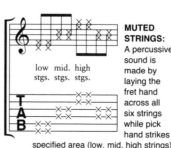

MUTED STRINGS: A percussive sound is made by laying the fret hand across all six strings while pick hand strikes specified area (low, mid, high strings).

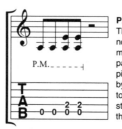

PALM MUTE: The note or notes are muted by the palm of the pick hand by lightly touching the string(s) near the bridge.

TREMOLO PICKING: The note or notes are picked as fast as possible.

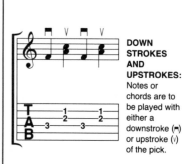

TRILL: Hammer on and pull off consecutively and as fast as possible between the original note and the grace note.

ACCENT: Notes or chords are to be played with added emphasis.

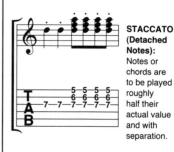

STACCATO (Detached Notes): Notes or chords are to be played roughly half their actual value and with separation.

DOWN STROKES AND UPSTROKES: Notes or chords are to be played with either a downstroke (⊓) or upstroke (∨) of the pick.

VIBRATO: The pitch of a note is varied by a rapid shaking of the fret hand finger, wrist, and forearm.

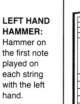